HARAKIRI

Elias Petropoulos

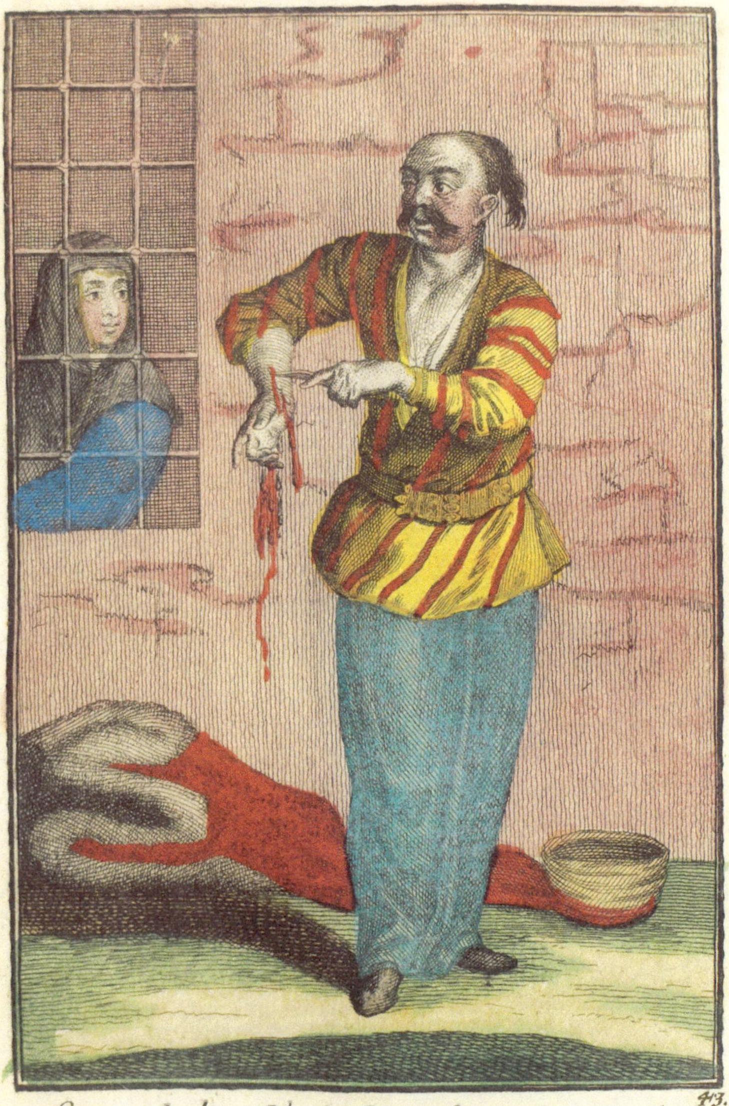

43.

Ein verliebter Türcke, der ſich in Arm ſticht
umb ſeiner Geliebten ein Probe von ſeiner Liebe Zu geben

HARAKIRI

Notes + Sketches / Averoff prison / 1969

ELIAS PETROPOULOS

Harakiri

The *mánges* (or tough lads) who resort to the practice of harakiri are called *harakírides.* And when I say "harakiri" I refer to the lacerations they make with a blade, on their arms and stomach, and more rarely on their throats.

The practice of harakiri, in its contemporary form, is a post-war phenomenon. Members of the underworld perform harakiri in order to deal with unbearable difficulties, or as a display of bravado. These difficulties take many forms: torturing by the police; prolonged, unlawful detention in holding-cells; and brutal solitary confinement (the inmate is completely naked, starved, and held in absolute darkness).

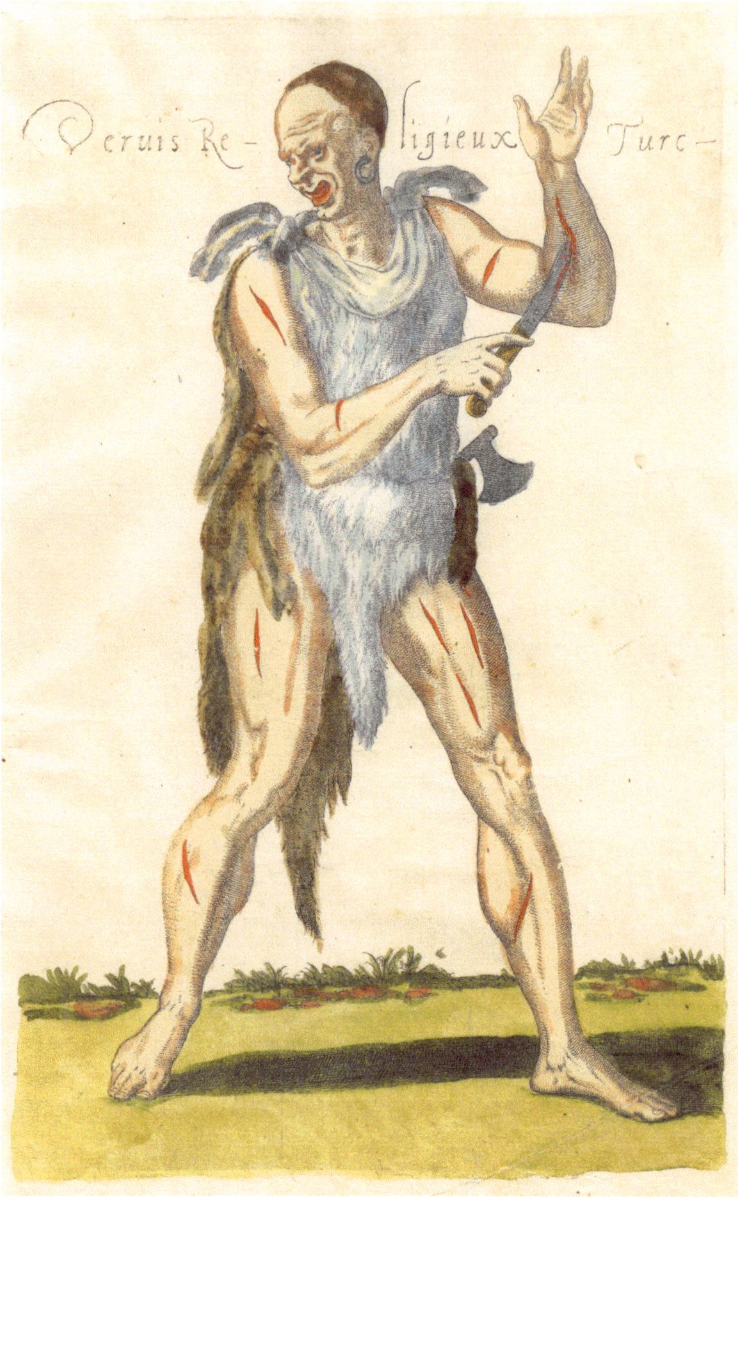
Deruis Re- ligieux Turc-

Harakiri also made its appearance in the army, where it was utilised by various young *mánges* (especially junkies) so that they could score a discharge or be granted leave.

Harakiri is characteristically practiced by the young. The older *mánges* and prison veterans hold the practice of harakiri in contempt and disdain.

When performed as a display of bravado, harakiri greatly resembles the older practice of *anália*, which we borrowed from the Turkish *kabadayi* and *zeybeks*.

In older times, the *koutsavákides*, when they danced, thrusted their dagger into their thighs and heels—here I describe something which I saw with my own eyes. It is in this corresponding tradition that the young *mánges* of today continue, who perform harakiri while dancing out a *zeybékiko*. Likewise, they also perform harakiri to impress the ladies. All this, of course, happens in the hardcore *skyládika* clubs, and not in the *koládika* clubs, which are frequented by pansies and wimps.

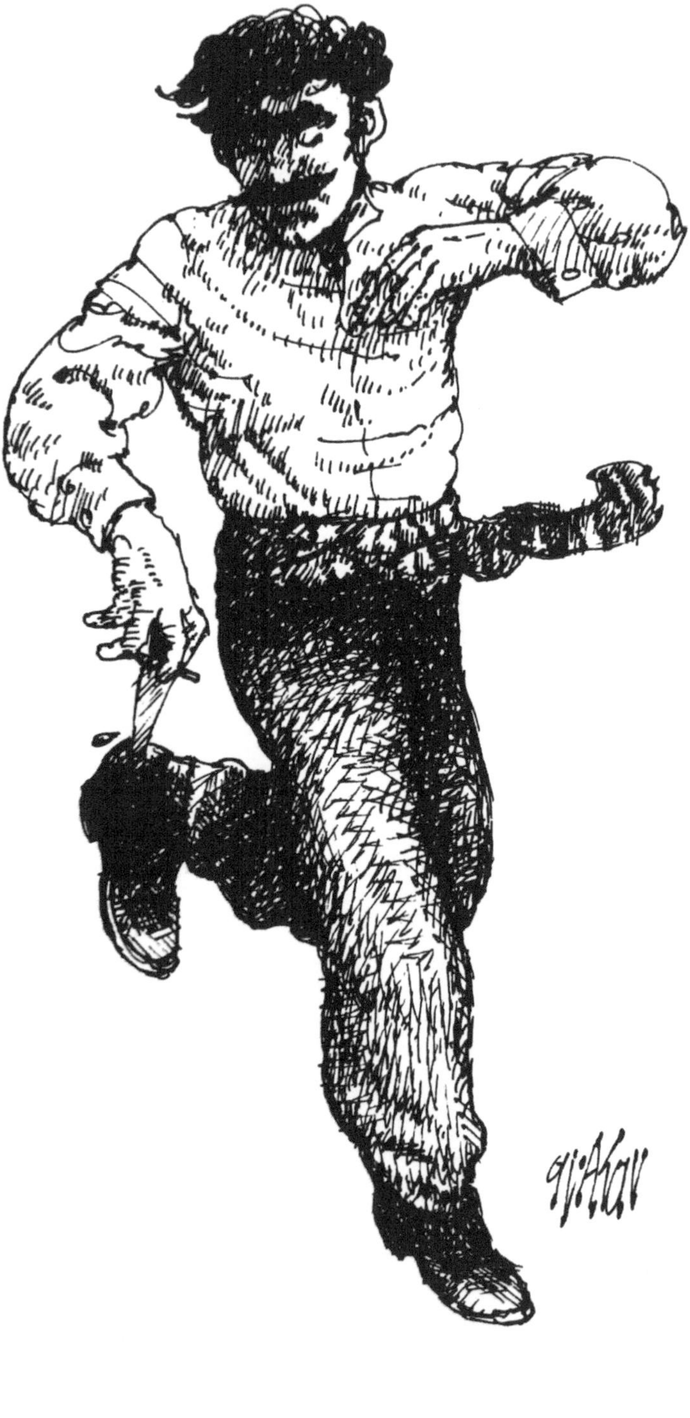

The technique of harakiri is simple. The *harakíris* takes a blade, or a small piece of blade, and makes a few lacerations, from which blood runs quickly and strongly. The lacerations are completely superficial, because the user holds the blade in such a way that only the tip of the blade sticks out. In the beginning, the practice of harakiri so terrified the torturers that they immediately stopped torturing their victims. They later learned, however, that this was a trick, and shouted at the *harakíris*: "*drop dead, you old faggot!*"

The practice of harakiri on the throat is truly spectacular. The *harakíris* pinches the skin of the throat with two fingers and makes two-to-three lacerations, giving the impression that he has been bloodily slaughtered. The lacerations made by the *harakíris* heal quickly. The scars which remain are called *tsaboukádes* (tattoos), or simply *xirafiés* (razor blade cuts).

When prisoners find a blade, they usually break it up into small pieces and hide it under the collar of their jacket, which they unstitch as needed. Junkies bury a piece of broken-up blade in their mouths so that when they start a fight they can draw it out quickly and slash the faces of their opponents. As you can see, junkies are particularly sneaky. Prisoners who languish in solitary confinement perform harakiri with a nail, or a shard of glass, or with the sawed-off top of a tin can.

The *daïdes* (or bully boys) butted out—and perhaps still butt out—cigarettes on their arms. For this reason, the undersides of their forearms were always full of pockmarks. Likewise, on the arms of prisoners one can see a variety of tattoos, which are also called *tsaboukádes* by the inmates. Some *mánges* later regret the tattoos which they have inked on their body and try to remove them: with cosmetic surgery, fig juice, or with citric acid. Some inmates obtain a piece of tripe from the prison kitchen, which they stick to a bandage and place on top of the tattoo. However odd this may seem, the tripe manages to remove the tattoo.

Here, I must mention the practice of *psaráki* (lit. little fish) which is one method of semi-suicide. Often, members of the underworld will build up momentum and smash their heads onto the walls of their cell, or onto the glass partitions of a police station interrogation room. That is the practice of *psaráki*. There have been occasions when a *mángas* has died from *psaráki*, wherein his head split open like a watermelon.

Don't bother searching in the phony slang lexicon of Zachos/Papazachariou to find the words I have mentioned: *harakiri / harakíris / anália / koládiko / xirafiés / tsaboukádes (tattoos) / psaráki*. You won't find them.

Paris, 11-4-2000.

Elias Petropoulos.

Note: This article is based on the notes (and later sketches) which Petropoulos kept in Averoff Prison, on 20-7-1969. It was first published in *Κυριακάτικη Ελευθεροτυπία* (Sunday Free Press), on 4-6-2000 and later anthologised in *Καπανταήδες και Μαχαιροβγάλτες* (Knives and Pistols), Nefeli Editions, 2001, pg 35-36.

Notes + Sketches
Averoff Prison (1969)

harakiri

for the Rebetika Songs Archive

notes + sketches

Averoff Prison

20-7-1969

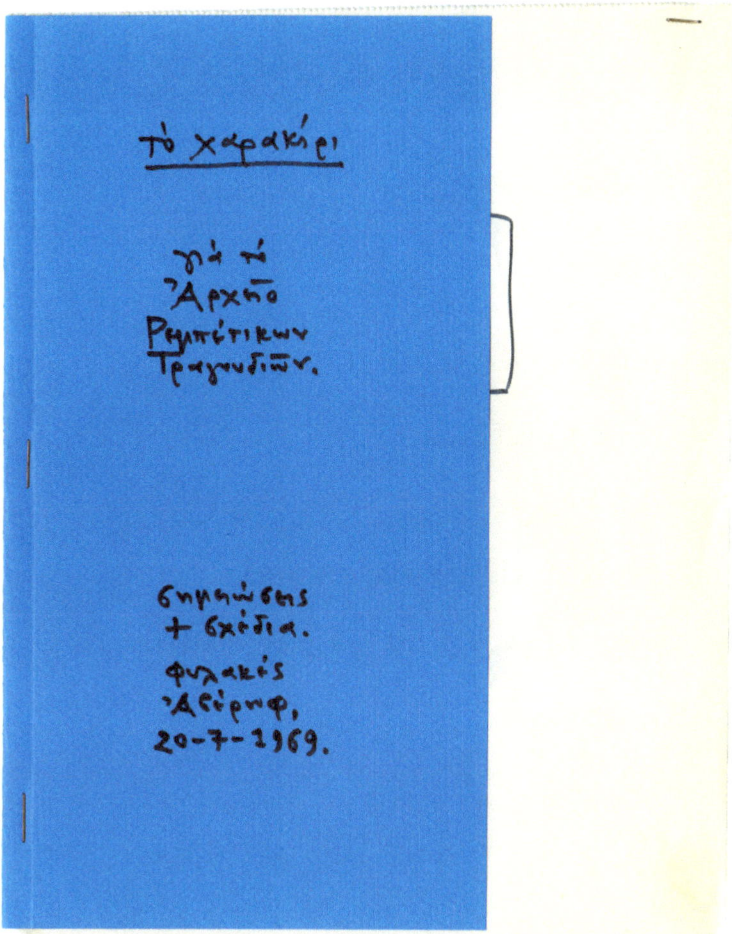
τὸ χαρακίρι
γιά τό
Ἀρχεῖο
Ρεμπέτικων
Τραγουδιῶν.
σημειώσεις
+ σχέδια.
φυλακές
Ἀβέρωφ,
20-7-1969.

Averoff Prison, 20-7-1969

HARAKIRI

Also called *tsaboukádes*

and *xirafiés*

Practiced on the arms (mainly the right)

and on the stomach

which bleed strongly, but harmlessly—

to cope with **difficulties** and

more rarely as a display of **bravado**

Difficulties:

custody (police)

prison (so that he can go to hospital)

holding cell

solitary confinement

army (for discharge or to be granted leave)

For bravado:

in a public space (for bravado, manliness)

for a woman

while dancing

Φυλακές Αβέρωφ, 20-7-1969.

ΧΑΡΑΚΙΡΙ

Τά λένε καί τσαμπουκάδες
ή ξυραφιές

Γίνονται στά μπράτσα (κυρίως στό δεξί)
καί στήν κοιλιά
απ' όπου τρέχει ακινδύνως άφθονο αίμα

Όταν αντιμετωπίζεις δυσκολία καί
σπανιώτερα γιά φιγούρα

Δυσκολία	Φιγούρα
Κρατητήρια (ασφάλεια)	σέ κέντρο (γιά μαγκιά)
Φυλακή (γιά νά πάει σέ νοσοκομείο)	σέ γκόμενα
Πειθαρχείο	σέ χορό
Απομόνωση	
Στρατό (γιά απαλλαγή γιά νά πάρει άδεια)	

δέν τούς
ὑπολήπτονται

Harakiri a post-war phenomenon.

It was directed at the police of the *Genikí Asfália* who were terrified by it.

Blood flows quickly and strongly.

Later they learned this was a trick and weren't frightened of the *harakírides*.

The prison veterans and the old *mánges* hold harakiri in contempt and disdain.

In olden times, they used to thrust knives into their thighs and heels.

One form of harakiri (*psaráki*): when the inmate smashes his head on the glass partition of the interrogation room or hits his head on the wall.

Τό χαρακίρι μεταπολεμικό φαινόμενο. Οἱ ἀστυνομικοί τῆς Γ.Α., ἐναντίον τῶν ὁποίων (ἔμμεσα) ἐστρέφετο, κυριολεκτικῶς ἐτρομοκρατοῦντο. Τά αἵματα ἔτρεχαν κρουνηδόν. Ἀργότερα ἔμαθαν τό κόλπο καί δέν τούς φόβιζαν οἱ χαρακίρηδες. Οἱ παλιοί κατάδικοι καί οἱ παλιοί μάγκες ἀγνοοῦν καί περιφρονοῦν τό χαρακίρι. Οἱ παλιοί κάρφωναν μαχαίρια στά μπούτια καί στίς φτέρνες τους. Μιά μορφή χαρακίρι: ὅταν ὁ κρατούμενος πέφτει μέ τό κεφάλι στήν τζαμαρία τοῦ ἀνακριτοῦ ἤ χτυπάει τό κεφάλι του στόν τοῖχο.

Ψαράκη

Pockmarks from butting out cigarettes
on the arms

Tattoos are removed:
with cosmetic surgery
with citric acid
with fig juice
with tripe

Οὐλές ἀπό σβησίματα τσιγάρων
στά μπράτσα

Τά τατουάζ σβήνουν:

μέ αἰσθητική ἐγχείρηση
μέ λεμόντζου (ξυνό)
μέ ὀπό συκιάς

} μέ πατσά

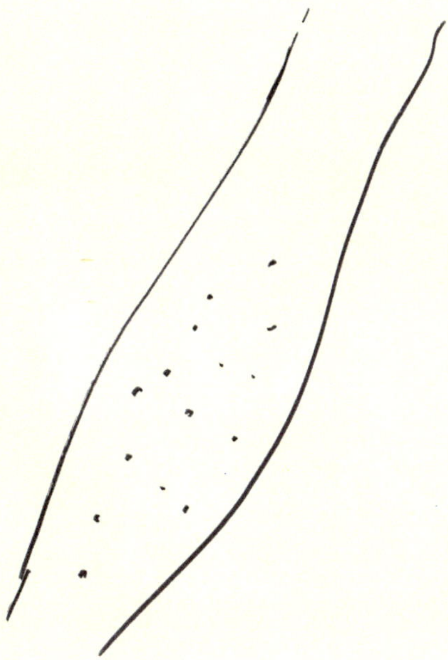

they hold the blade like this

so that only the tip can be seen

---

in the holding-cell harakiri

is practiced with a

shard of glass

nail

sheet metal

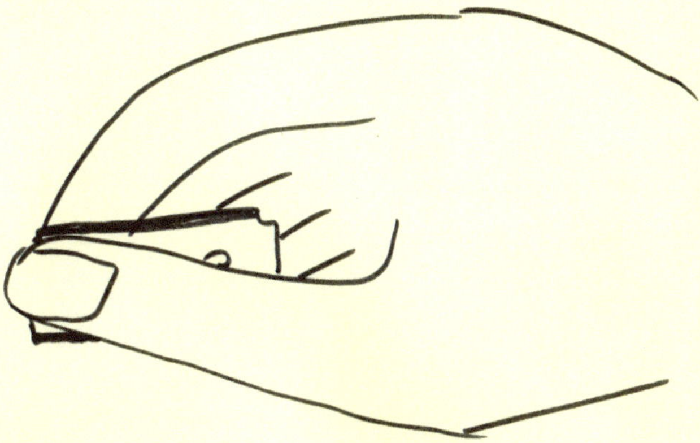

Ἔτσι κρατοῦν τό ξυραφάκι
ὥστε νά φαίνεται μόνον ὁ ἀθέρας.

Στό πειθαρχεῖο τό χαρακίρι
γίνεται καί μέ γιαλί
καρφί
λαμαρίνα

crosswise cuts———————————parallel cuts

horizontal cuts on the stomach

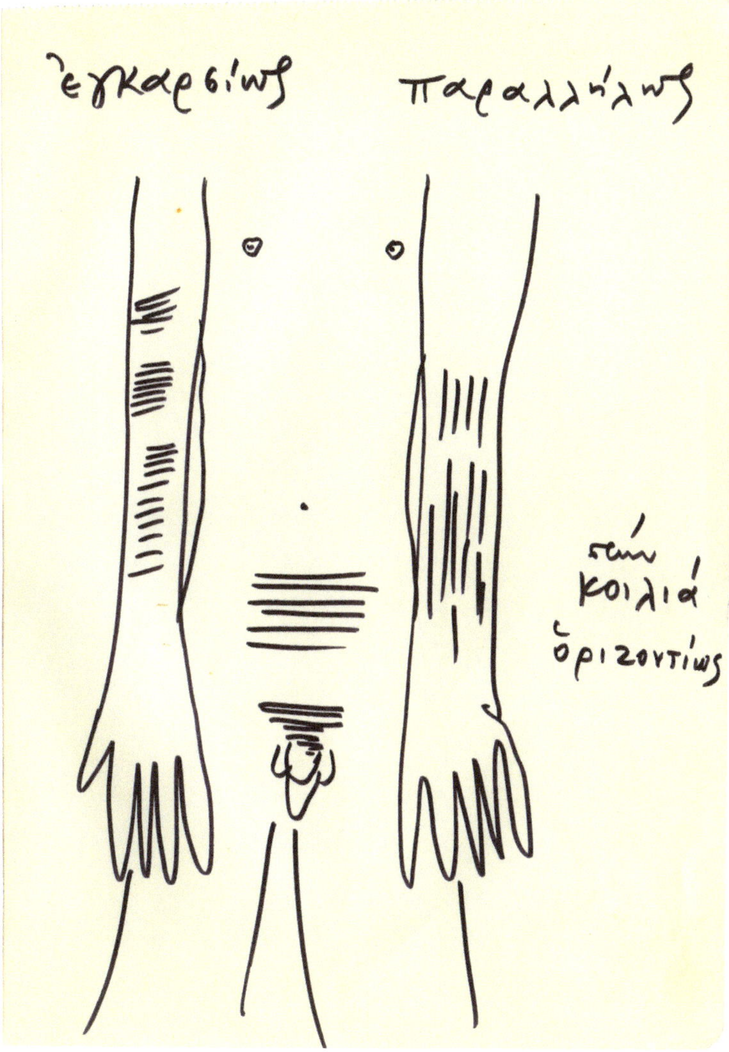
ἐγκαρσίως
παραλλήλως
στήν
κοιλιά
ὁριζοντίως

Prison Drawings

1. *Junkie cutting himself with a razor blade*, 1969, Averoff Prison (?).

Junkies — when they grab and pinch the skin of the throat, they stretch it and then slice it with a small blade.

Blood flows plentifully, but it does no harm —they look slaughtered.

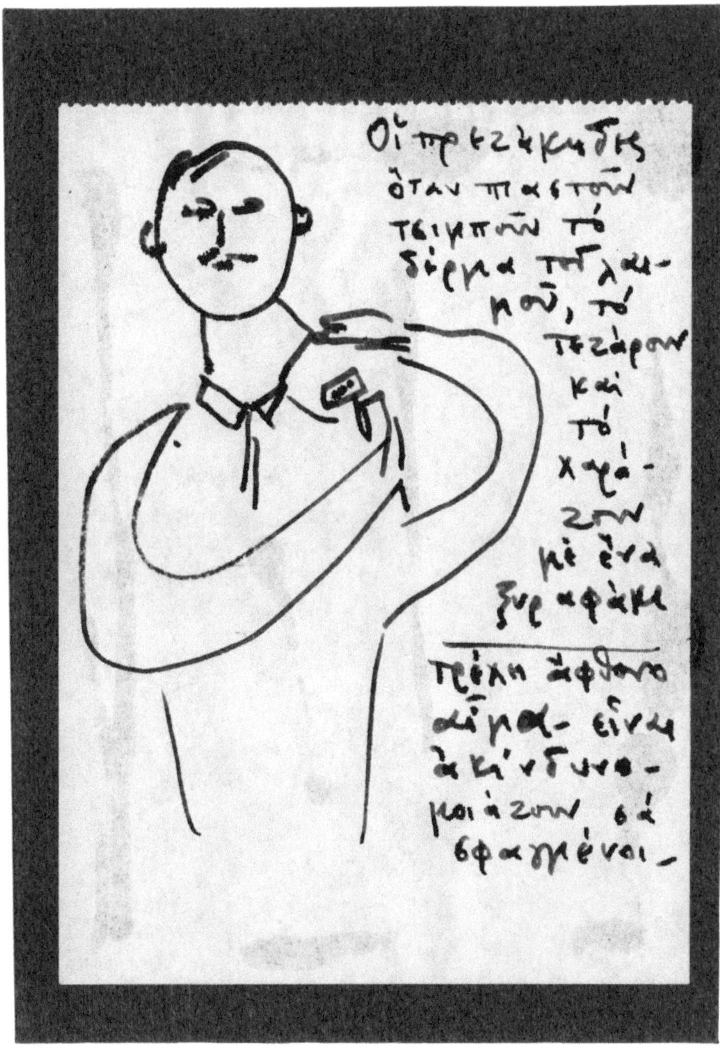
Οἱ πρεζάκηδες
ὅταν πιαστοῦν
τσιμποῦν τό
δέρμα τοῦ λαι-
μοῦ, τό
τεζάρουν
καί
τό
χαρά-
ζουν
μέ ἕνα
ξυραφάκι
τρέχει ἄφθονο
αἷμα- εἶναι
ἀκίνδυνο-
μοιάζουν σά
σφαγμένοι-

2. *A heroin addict*, undated, Averoff Prison (?).

A heroin addict with wooden splints in his eyes so that they can stay open.

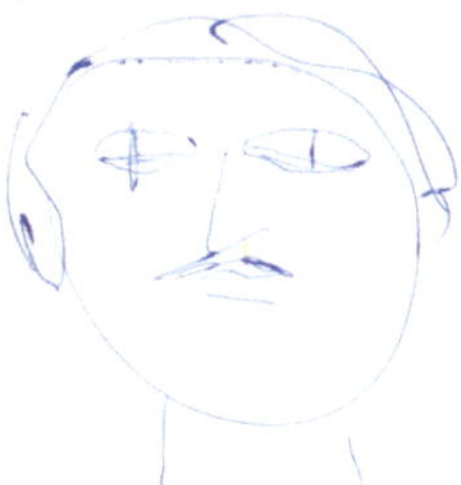

φύλακας μὲ σπιρτόξυλα
στὰ μάτια γιὰ νὰ
στέκουν ἀνοιχτά.

3a. *Prison snitch with scar on his cheek*, 1969, Averoff Prison (?).

the snitches (traitors)

they slice on the cheek.

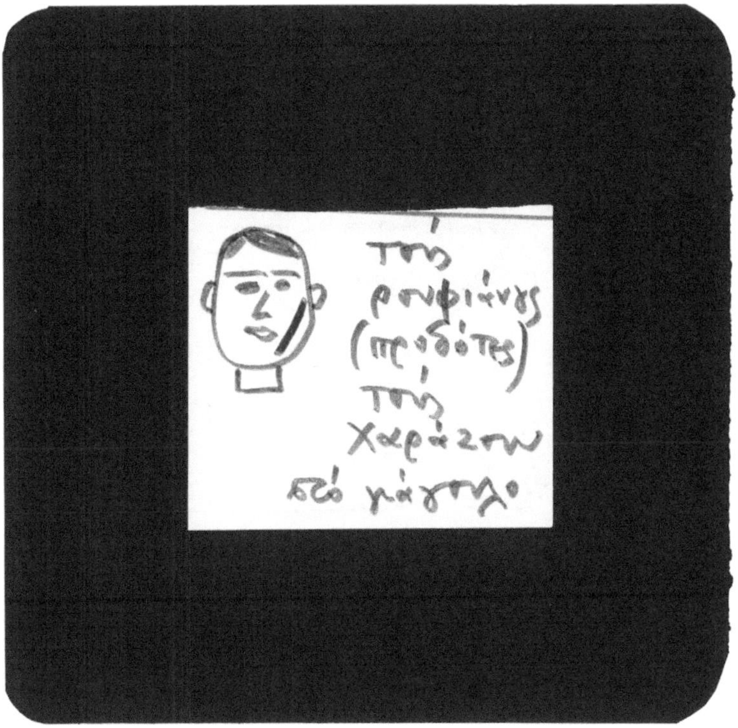
Τότε
ρουφιάνους
(προδότες)
τότε
χαράζουν
στό μάγουλο

3b. *Sfregio*, illustration by Manuel Orazi in *Je sais tout* (April 15, 1910).

A young Camorra endures the *sfregio*, a mark of dishonour which is slashed on the cheek. This practice of dishonourable punishment by the Camorra also made its way to Greece, where the *mánges* give the following threat: beware, cos I'll take down ya mug!

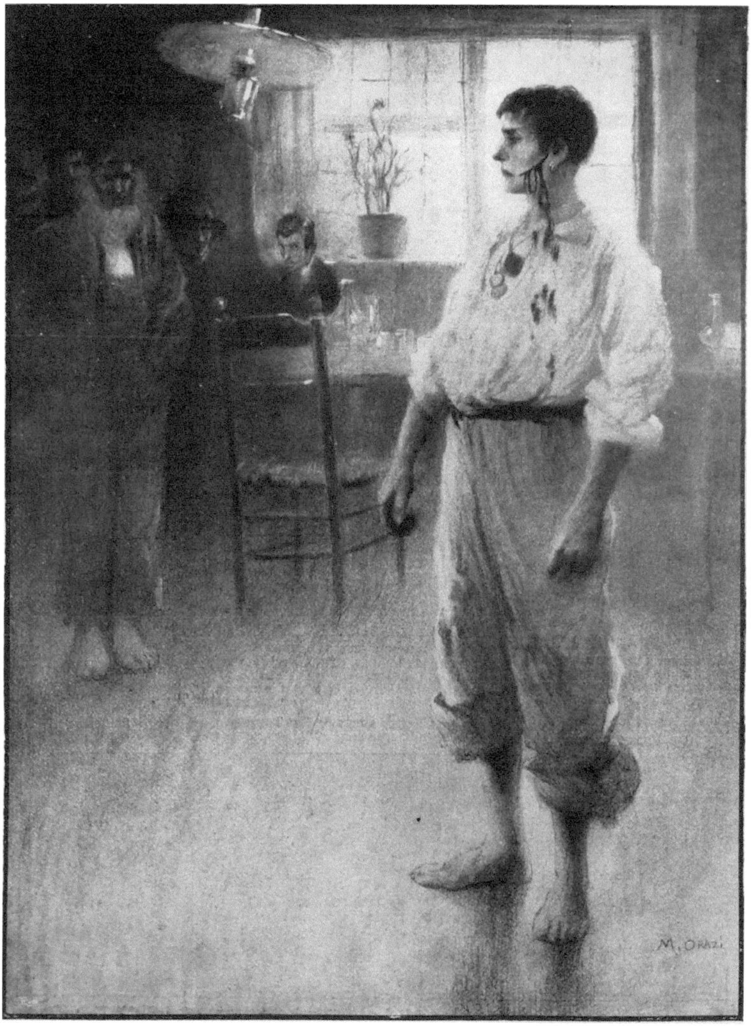
M. ORAZI

4. *Prison torture sketches*, undated, Averoff Prison (?).

torture bench

hoisting apparatus with pulley

[Notes: Sketches that I made in prison from hearing about scenes of torture carried out by the police. On the bench they battered the soles of the feet (*fálagga*): a method of torture whereby the feet are tied and continuously beaten.

On the pulley hoist they hang you by the wrists. Siklís was hung and left starving for 39 hours].

πάγκος ἐργασίας

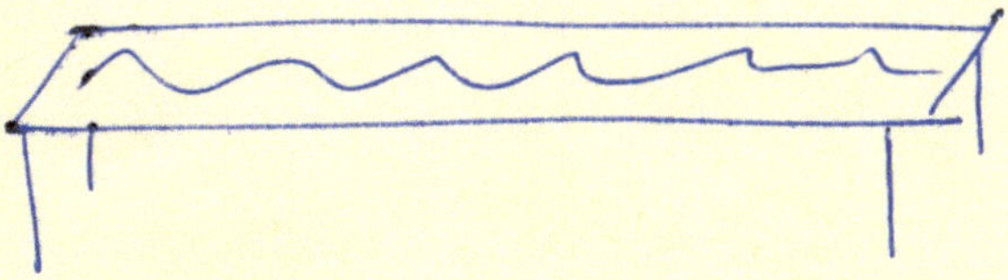

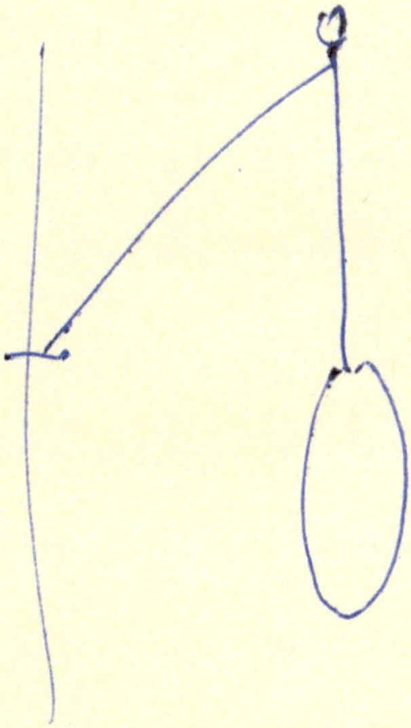

πρόχειρο
παλάγκο
μέ μιά
τροχαλία

5. *Prison tin-can ashtray*, undated, Averoff Prison (?).

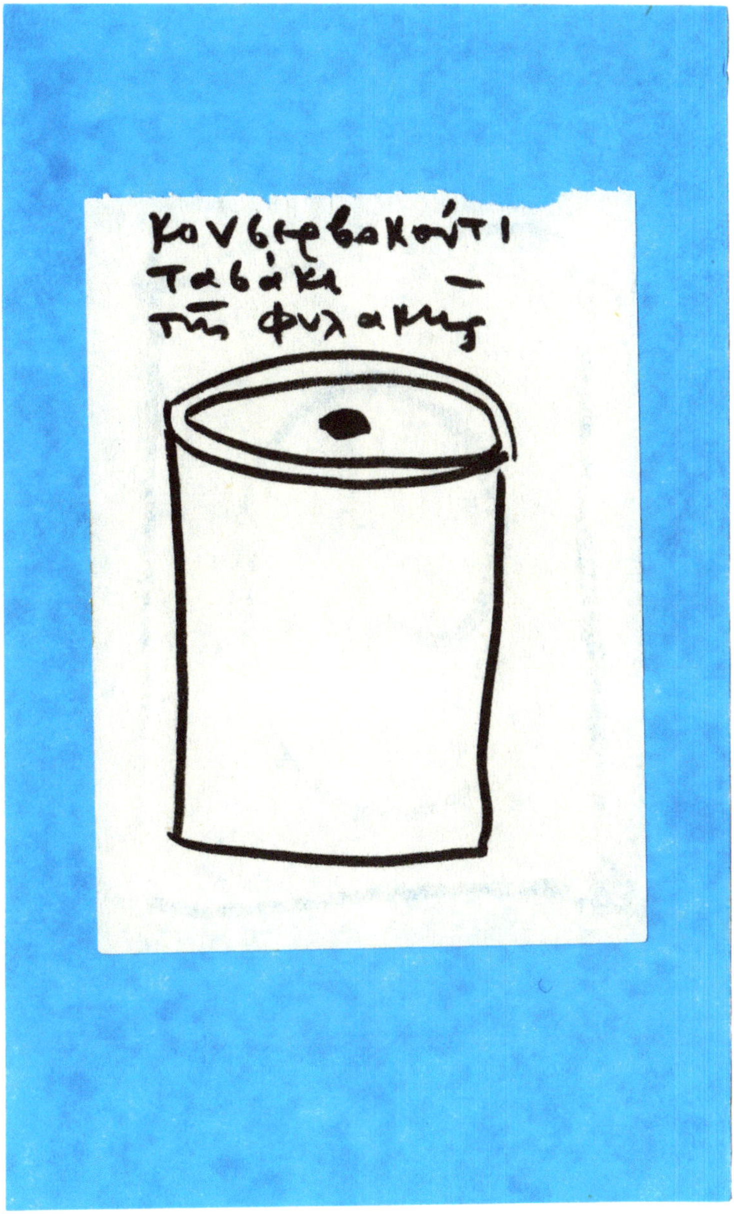
κονσερβοκούτι
ταβάκι
της φυλακής

6. *Prison cell chamber pot*, 1969, Averoff Prison.

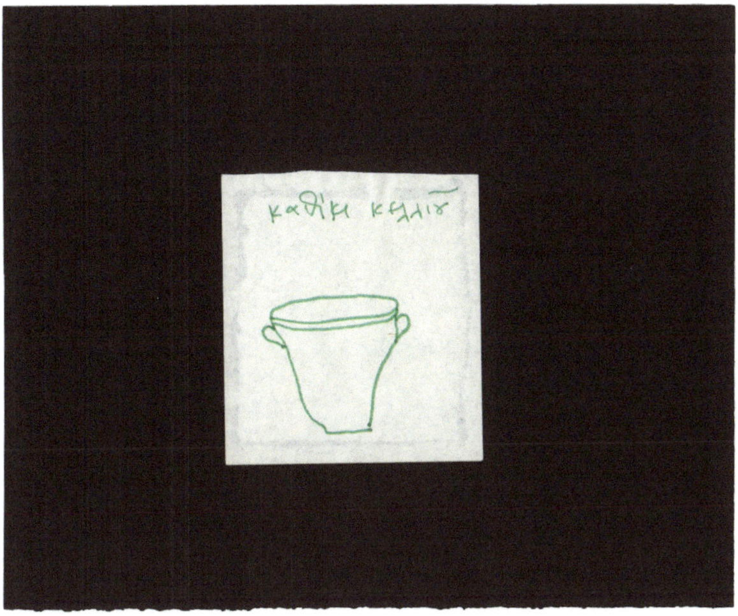

7. *Cell in Averoff Prison,* July 1969.

To see outside the window one had to climb on top of the bedside table.

κελί στίς φυλακές Ἀβέρωφ — Ἰούλιος '69

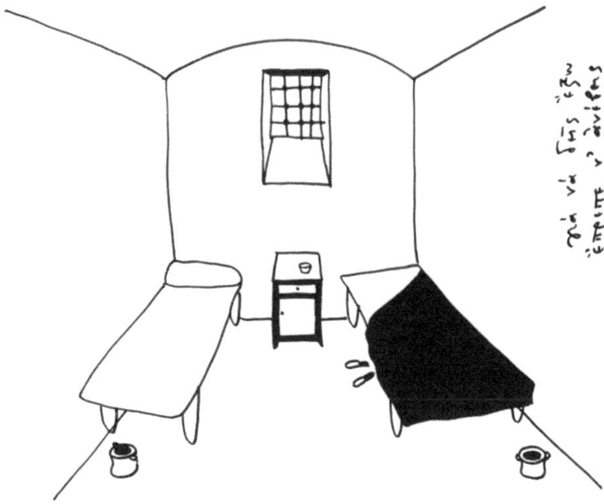

γιά νά δεῖς ἔξω
ἔπρεπε ν' ἀνέβεις
πάνω στό κομοδίνο.

Notes

Harakiri (notes + sketches) Averoff Prison, 20-7-1969

Stapled booklet held in the Elias Petropoulos papers at the Gennadius Library, Athens:

Section IV - Visual Material, Box 3, Folder 5.

Prison Drawings

1. *Junkie cutting himself with a razor blade*, 1969, Averoff Prison (?). Courtesy of the Gennadius Library, Athens, Elias Petropoulos papers: Section II - Personal Items, Box 4.

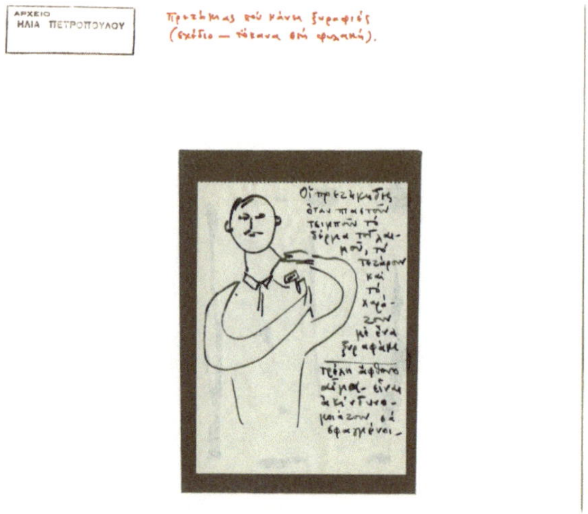

2. *A heroin addict*, undated, Averoff Prison (?). Courtesy of the Gennadius Library, Athens, Elias Petropoulos papers: Section II - Personal Items, Box 4.

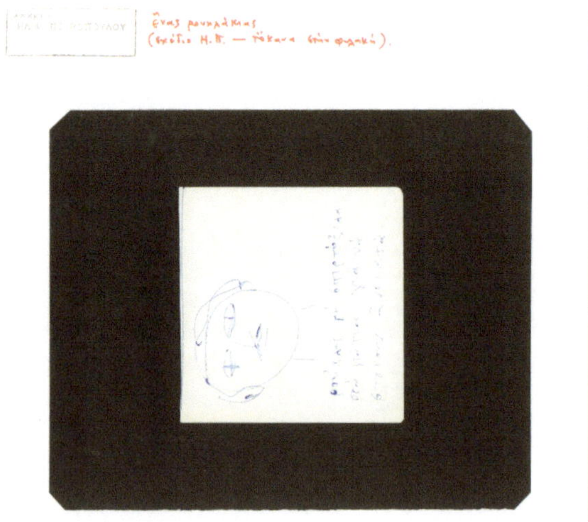

3a. *Prison snitch with scar on his cheek*, 1969, Averoff Prison (?). Courtesy of the Gennadius Library, Athens, Elias Petropoulos papers: Section II - Personal Items, Box 4.

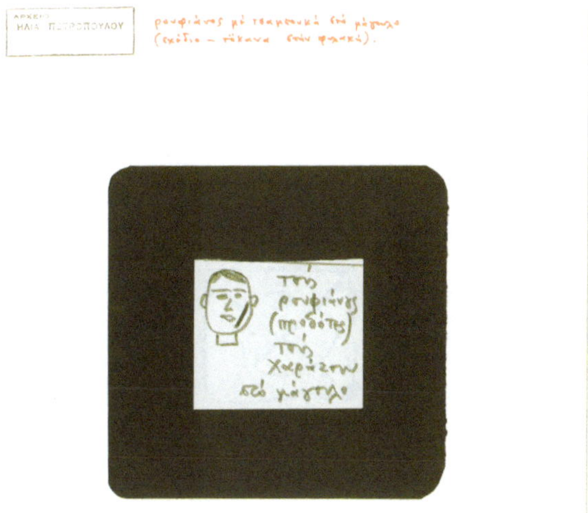

3b. *Sfregio*, illustration by Manuel Orazi in *Je sais tout: magazine encyclopédique illustré*, (April 15, 1910), pg 324.

Note by Elias Petropoulos in *Το Άγιο Χασισάκι* (Holy Hashish), Nefeli Publishing, 1991, pg 227.

4. *Prison torture sketches*, undated, Averoff Prison (?) Courtesy of the Gennadius Library, Athens, Elias Petropoulos papers: Section IV - Visual Material, Box 3, Folder 5.

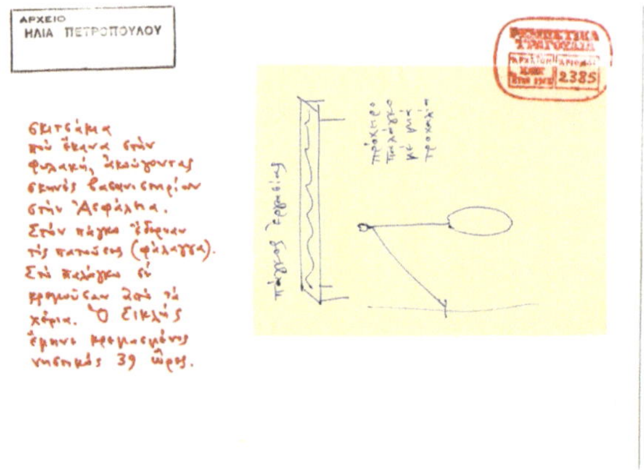

5. *Prison tin-can ashtray*, undated, Averoff Prison (?). Courtesy of the Gennadius Library, Athens, Elias Petropoulos papers: Section II - Personal Items, Box 4.

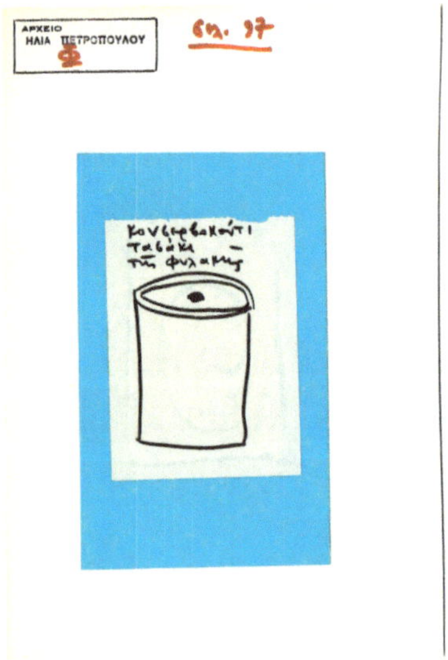

6. *Prison cell chamber pot*, 1969, Averoff Prison. Courtesy of the Gennadius Library, Athens, Elias Petropoulos papers: Section II - Personal Items, Box 4.

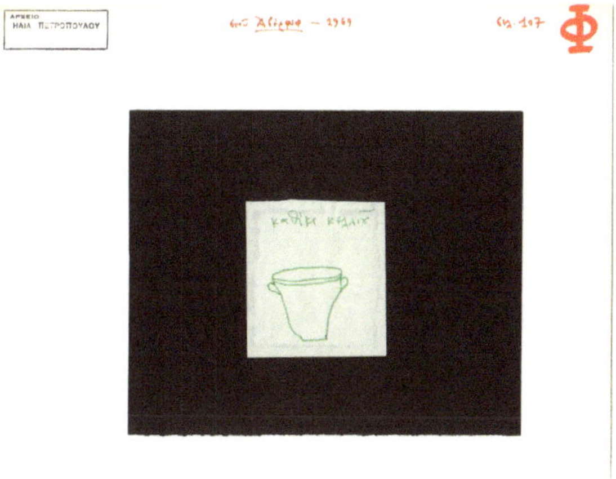

7. *Cell in Averoff Prison*, July 1969. Courtesy of the Gennadius Library, Athens, Elias Petropoulos papers: Section II - Personal Items, Box 4.

Edited and translated by Michael Alexandratos.

Nefeli Editions (Athens, Greece) published the article «οι χαρακίρηδες» in *Καπανταήδες και Μαχαιροβγάλτες* (Knives and Pistols), 2001.

Image credits:

pg iv - Engraving of a Turkish man cutting his arm in full view of his lover, based on a painting by Jean-Baptiste Vanmour (1671-1737).

pg 2 - Dervis, Religieux Turc, *Les quatre premiers livres des navigations et pérégrinations orientales*, 1568, Nicolas de Nicolay (author), Louis Danet (engraver), Lyon: G. Roville (publisher). Hand-coloured engraving in the collection of the editor.

pg 4 - Drawing of a *mangas* sticking a dagger in his heel, by Anakreon Kanavakis.

Published by Cycladic Press, (Sydney, Australia).

ISBN: 978-0-646-89479-9

cycladic.press@gmail.com

www.ingramcontent.com/pod-product-compliance
Ingram Content Group UK Ltd.
Pitfield, Milton Keynes, MK11 3LW, UK
UKHW061029310726
14089UKWH00018B/259/J

* 9 7 8 0 6 4 6 8 9 4 7 9 9 *